SIMPLE GUIDES

S0-BYN-845

CUSTOMS & ETIQUETTE OF
FRANCE

ABOUT THE AUTHOR

DANIELLE ROBINSON was born and bred in the South of France, (Toulouse), but has lived in England since her twenties. Subsequently, she taught French throughout the UK and brought up a family. Today she is Honorary Senior Visiting Fellow at the University of Bradford as well as part-time lecturer at the University of Wales, Lampeter. She has an interest in contemporary French culture, especially its North African component; she is author of *The Simple Guide to Islam*. She is also an accomplished interpreter and is sometimes available to take visiting parties to France. She can be contacted through her e-mail address: daniellerobinson@onetel.net.uk.

For René Marre, my very French father.
For Neal, my husband, an English perfectionist who can also call the cows in Occitan, thereby contributing greatly to European Entente Cordiale.
For Zoé and Eléonor, who share, if nothing else, the thrilling encumberance of being 'Franglaise'.

ILLUSTRATED BY
IRENE SANDERSON

CUSTOMS & ETIQUETTE OF
FRANCE

Danielle Robinson

Customs & Etiquette of France
by Danielle Robinson

First published 1992 by Global Books Ltd.
Second edition 1998, Third edition 2001
This edition published 2005 by
Simple Guides an imprint of Bravo Ltd.
59 Hutton Grove
London N12 8DS
Tel: +44 (0) 208 446 2440
Fax: +44 (0) 208 446 2441
Enquiries: sales@bravo.clara.net

ISBN 1-85733-388-8

British Library Cataloguing in Publication Data
A CIP catalogue entry for this book
is available from the British Library

Cover image: ©Dave Saunders / www.travel-ink.co.uk
Set in Futura 11 on 12 pt by Bookman, Hayes
Printed and bound in China

Contents

Foreword
– TO SECOND EDITION –

France is a fascinating country. You know this already and have now decided to go and see for yourself properly, not just as a hurried tourist shepherded by a travel firm's representative. You may be going there on business, or wondering whether it is at all possible to do business there; or you may be going for the most important business of all, your own business, on whatever quest or dream you wish to pursue. In order to be successful, you will need to interact with the French.

Unless you speak their language perfectly, you will be perceived as a *foreigner* and excuses will therefore be made for your 'odd' behaviour. That does not mean, however, that you should feel or be made to feel an *outsider*.

The aim of this fully revised guide is to bring you up to date with recent developments in French society and to enable you to gain access to a culture and way of life which started flourishing in Gallo-Roman times about two thousand years ago and is forever changing as it faces up to the impact of a united Europe and globalization.

This is only a simple introduction to a huge and diverse topic, but the hope is that it will make you feel more at ease with the customs and etiquette of a very varied nation. The wonderful thing is that nobody understands the French perfectly and they seem always to disagree amongst themselves – disparaging their achievements at the same time as they praise them. International experts say that they only do this because they are so interested in themselves. Frustrating? No, fascinating! So take heart and enjoy France.

DANIELLE ROBINSON,

Foreword to the Third Edition

It has been my pleasure, ever since finishing the 1998 edition, to think of what I would really like to pass on to English-speaking readers planning to go to France. It will not be many new facts I will add but more of an approach to life in France.

Some facts have actually been removed from the earlier text. Does it matter whether you know that roses are bought in odd numbers (except 13). My own experience of buying flowers in France, even cheap ones, is that florists know their job. They would not dream of thrusting into your hands a bunch roughly wrapped in what looks like Granny's old wallpaper. Unasked, they invent a wrapping to match your chosen flowers, which become a double delight to keep for yourself, or give.

For an approach to life, my great discoveries have been two authors whom I knew from other writings. The way in which they have understood France and are passing it on in English, strikes deep chords with a French woman who, from Britain also, meditates on the country she chose to leave, possibly to love it at a distance. So let me first quote here a few lines from Theodore Zeldin's wonderful *An Intimate History of Humanity*:[1]

> Freud wrote about humanity on the basis of meetings with patients largely from one country, even if he did drape an oriental carpet over his couch. I had long conversations with people of eighteen different nationalities in the course of my research, and started each chapter with witnesses from a different part of the world, but I did not want to suggest that any particular country might somehow be more liable to a particular worry or weakness. The majority of the living characters in this book, therefore, also come from a single country. It is a rich one (though it knows poverty too), a free country (but one struggling against many subtle restrictions), a favourite for tourists because of its devotion to the good life, attracting as many each year as it has inhabitants, but nevertheless not finding living all that simple, and it

is probably disliked by quite as many foreigners as admire it. I am thus able to ask what there is left for humans to do, once they have won their basic comforts and their freedom, or at least some freedoms.

I met most of these women in France, a country which has been like a laboratory for me for all my adult life, a constant source of inspiration. All my books on France have been attempts to understand the art of life, by the light of the fireworks which that country sends into the sky in its effort to understand itself. What I value particularly is its tradition of thinking about its own problems in universal terms, and, self-absorbed though it is, of going beyond the self-preoccupation which all nations feel. The Declaration of the Rights of Man was made on behalf of the entire world. It seems to me that any new vision of the future must, more than ever before, include the whole of humanity, and that is why I have written my book this way.

This new edition for 2001 onwards is my chance, for what I aim to recreate, first in the following pages and then when you actually set foot in France, is akin to the shared delight of a bouquet.

DANIELLE ROBINSON

1. Vintage, 1998. ISBN 0-7493-962-37

Getting to Know France

'. . .a great variety of culture, customs and culinary traditions'

Excluding Russia, France is the largest country in Europe (551,602km^2, including Corsica) but with a population of 58 million it is, in fact, one of the least densely populated. There are many large towns and cities but also vast rural areas with very few inhabitants and, in some regions, villages have been abandoned. In recent years, Europeans from more crowded countries such as Germany, Great Britain or the Netherlands have bought these abandoned houses, including many farmhouses, which are often situated in areas of breathtaking beauty.

The Regions of France

The locals are intrigued with such activity and follow the enthusiastic arrival of removal vans with some amusement, wondering how long the fad will last. Although prices can be much lower than for a similar property in, say, the UK, solicitor's fees (*frais de notaire*) are high. French banks can be helpful in providing French mortgages and also guidelines from their London offices. It is also advisable to make enquiries from the town hall (*mairie*) of your dream village. But beware, too many such dreams have already ended in nightmares.

The shape of France is roughly that of a hexagon and French people very often use this term when they refer to their country. The other term besides 'l'Hexagone' is 'la France métropolitaine' or just 'la métropole' which has nothing to do with le métro (the tube, subway). It rather signals the difference between *la mère patrie* (bring in the psychiatrist as you try and translate this motto into the 'mother fatherland'!) and the colonies, or what is left of them in the form of *DOM* or *TOM* (*Départements d'outre mer* and *Territoires d'outre mer* = overseas).

Three of the sides of the hexagon of course can clearly be seen to be coastlines (the Channel, the Atlantic Ocean to the west and the Mediterranean to the south-east), and one side is a mountain range, (the *Pyrénées*; literally 'born of fire') separating France from Spain. Another side is made up of mountains (the Alps and Jura separating France from Italy and Switzerland) and part of the river Rhine, (a border with Germany). The North-East is the only side not to have natural frontiers with its neighbours (Germany, Luxemburg and Belgium).

There is a great diversity of landscape and variations in climate. In the northern and western parts the sea ensures mild winters but the eastern regions have a harsher climate of a more continental nature. On the Mediterranean coast people enjoy very mild winters but the summers can be unbearably hot, with a risk of drought and forest fires. Mont Blanc in the French Alps is the highest peak in Europe (4867m.=15,771ft.).

Although France has been a unified and very centralized country for centuries, its regions have retained a great variety of culture, customs and culinary traditions.

For administrative purposes France is divided into 100 *départements* (96 in the *métropole* and 4 DOM) which are grouped into 26 *régions* (22 in l'Hexagone and 4 DOM). *Départements* are ordered alphabetically and numbered. These numbers are used as postal codes and as the last two digits of car registration numbers; for example 75 stands for Paris.

Départements were introduced after the 1789 revolution, but when asked where he comes from, a Frenchman will probably use the name of the pre-revolutionary province and proudly declare he was born in Brittany, Normandy or Provence, which are cultural entities. The names immediately conjure up a particular type of landscape, climate, traditions, specialities and way of speaking.

Hot Tip: To Comply or not to Comply. . .

Despite efforts at decentralization in recent years, the French administrative structure remains extremely centralized and hierarchical. Not surprisingly, therefore, it is a kind of national sport for the French to try to beat the system and avoid complying with decisions made in higher places. Behaviour which, in other countries, might be regarded as cheating, is looked on as perfectly acceptable. The attitude seems to be: Why should one obey silly regulations?

Rivers as well as mountains provide a useful way of quickly situating a town or area since a great many *départements* are named after them. You already know that Paris is **on** the SEINE (river) and **in** the Seine (*département* 75). You may enjoy following the course of the other great rivers (*fleuves*). France has five *fleuves* and a great many lesser *rivières*. You will have heard of the LOIRE, famous for its beautiful Renaissance châteaux and fine light wines. The area is also supposed to have the purest French accent and was certainly the heart of civilization in the sixteenth century.

The RHINE, as mentioned above, separates the province of Alsace from the Black Forest in Germany and was for long a bitterly disputed territory. The city of Strasb(o)urg now symbolizes the new era of peace with its European Parliament. The powerful RHÔNE, coming from Switzerland through Lake Geneva changes direction at **Lyon** and then flows south; **Marseille** is found on its Mediterranean delta.

The French spelling of these very important cities, second and third after Paris, does not include the -s found in the English spelling, which is always a source of puzzlement to the French for whom the -s marks the plural.

The GARONNE comes from Spain, changes direction at Toulouse then flows west towards the Atlantic where Bordeaux lies on its estuary called the Gironde. Toulouse and Bordeaux are fine southern cities, ranking fourth and fifth in France.

As in many countries, a North/South divide exists. Northerners think people from the *midi* (the South) talk and boast a lot, that they make friends very easily but that this friendliness is somewhat superficial. They reckon the southerners have a different conception of time and never hurry. On the other hand, southerners pity northerners for living in what to them seems a cold climate which affects their character. *Les gens du Nord* are described as cold, hard-working, not very sociable and difficult to make friends with – but when friendship develops, it is a deep and long-lasting relationship.

In recent years efforts have been made to give the REGIONS a greater say in the running of their own affairs, being reintroduced between 1972 and 1986 as larger administrative units to provide some sort of decentralization away from Paris and as a better framework for Europe. As they echo the old provinces, they are generally well accepted and the leader of the regional council is a powerful political figure.

2

France: A Brief History

From a painting by Delacroix (1830) – 'Liberty leading the People'

In accordance with the revised series, readers are to be provided with a few pages of history. France is an old country and even starting after the Roman conquest about 50 years BC, selection is difficult. The geographical borders of France have varied considerably as smaller kingdoms feuded, or associated under one ruler.

A list of kings would be tedious; there are no queens in France except as consorts or regents due to the 'Salic law', a Frankish institution barring women from reigning or passing on the right to the throne. This created many wars with countries, especially Britain, who considered French princesses as entitled to pass their rights to their British heirs!

The little Pyrencan kingdom of Navarre, where the Salic law did not apply, was also considered fair game for the French kings who married the female heiresses. It is an important little enclave around Foix, as it contributed the only Protestant king to the French crown (although he had to become a Catholic to reign, doing so with the mythical words, 'Paris is well worth a mass'.

Henry IV was responsible for a period of prosperity and peace after the wars of religion, establishing in 1598 the 'Edict of Nantes' which granted Protestants the right of worship and personal security. After his death, in 1610, caused by a traffic jam in Paris which allowed a fanatic to stab him to death as his carriage was stuck in the crowds, Protestant rights were consistently eroded until they disappeared with the catastrophic 'Revocation' of the edict in 1685, which instituted state persecution. This led to mass emigration of the Huguenots to the Netherlands, Britain (Petty France in London), Germany, and South Carolina.

In 1764, persecutions became less stringent in exchange for leniency towards French Catholic settlers in Canada, now lost by France to Britain. After American Independence (1783), Jefferson and La Fayette obtained official tolerance for French Protestants in 1788. By then time was running out for despotism and the revolutionary Declaration of the Rights of Man made all citizens equal notwithstanding their religion. In 1789, the Republican motto was born: Liberty, Equality, Fraternity. It adorns monuments, coins, schools and town halls throughout France.

ROMAN CONQUEST

After this foray into sixteenth-to-eighteenth-century France, let us have a quick flash-back to the Roman conquest. Some say it was an accident since Julius Caesar really wanted to be a commander on the Danube and not in the provincial backwaters of Gaul. Once there, however, his greed for local gold to pay off his huge debts and his lack of diplomatic skills landed Rome in a full-scale war. Since Rome won, the rest is history, but not completely laid to rest as you will know from the popularity of the various *Asterix* cartoon strips which have captured the imagination of twentieth-century France and a good part of the world too. Parc Asterix can be visited as a patriotic alternative to Disneyland! In the Asterix stories, we are made to believe that French brains always won against Roman brawn.

Visitors are strongly encouraged, however, to visit the actual historical Roman remains, mainly on the Mediterranean, such as the splendid aqueduct called Le Pont du Gard, the bullfighting arena in Nimes, and many other fine sights. If there is no time to go as far as Provence, the Musée de Cluny, in the heart of the Latin Quarter, which houses the magnificent medieval tapestry of 'The Lady and the Unicorn' and other medieval treasures, is based in an old Roman bath house.

If one tries to survey 2000 years of history in a few lines, one may as well be guided by what the natives remember as being their past. Some memories of olden times survive in children's traditional songs. Who cares for the 'Lazy Kings' dynasty around the seventh century? Yet ask anyone and they can sing:

> Le bon roi Dagobert (good old King Dagobert)
> Avait mis sa culotte à l'envers (had put his breeches on inside out)
> Le bon St Eloi (good St Eloi – Mayor of the palace/Prime Minister/Church official)
> Lui dit: 'Oh mon roi, (said to him; Oh my king)
> Votre Majesté/ est mal culottée (Your Royal Majesty/is not dressed properly)
> C'est vrai, lui dit le roi (Dear me said the King)
> Je vais la remettre à l'endroit (I'll go and straighten myself right now)

FROM CLOVIS TO CHARLEMAGNE

The official founder of the dynasty was Clovis who was the first Frankish king to become a Christian as his wife's God won the bet and gave him victory. He was subsequently baptised in Rheims by St Remi in 498/9. A visit to France by the present Pope to mark the 1500th anniversary was not appreciated by all French people since France is supposed to be a lay country. Although Clovis had been an active leader, his Merovingian successors preferred to enjoy life and leave the power to their palace officials, an early example of political 'cohabitation'? Eventually, the efficient mayors, the most famous of whom was Charles Martel because he stopped the Arab invasion from pushing further north than Poitiers in 732, became kings and formed their own lineage, the Carolingians, who include Charlemagne (Carolus Magnus).

Then the Capetian dynasty, supposedly the oldest-documented in the world, takes us towards the end of the Middle Ages when several Valois branches come to the fore because the only live child of a king is a girl and the Salic law applies. The Hundred-Year War with England occupies the period 1337-1453 during which troublesome Joan of Arc is sold to the English for 10,000 pounds and burnt alive in 1431 in Rouen. Then wars with Italy last over a half-century until 1560 when the wars of religion start. We have seen how Henry IV only temporarily unified France.

LOTS OF LOUIS

The long period of the powerful Louis started inauspiciously with the last rebellion of the high nobility against central power, but for good or bad, modern centralized France was in the making. Louis XIII, and his son Louis XIV who reigned seventy-three years until 1715, calling himself *Le Roi Soleil*, the Sun King, created the institutions for which France is still known, such as *l'Académie Francaise*. It was the golden age for classical drama, which you can still enjoy at its most stilted in the *Comédie Francaise* situated near Le Louvre, which was the achievement of the period until Louis XIV had *Versailles* built.

Because he reigned for so long and because his descendants died of poor medical care (this is the period when Molière wrote his satirical comedies against doctors and died on stage performing 'The Hypocondriac'), his successor Louis XV was his great-grandson. First called 'the beloved', he ended up being buried amongst angry demonstrations accused of having ruined France through his profligacy. His son Louis XVI fared even worse since he was beheaded in 1793 after the 1789 Revolution.

FROM RUINS TO RESTORATION

By 1799, France was really ruined, civil liberties suspended, and the 'nouveaux riches' experimented with extravagant costumes and frivolity to forget austerity and terror. A 'Consulate' system imitating Roman recipes for government was set up to improve matters. Napoleon Bonaparte was one of its three leaders and by 1804 had become Emperor. The Pope even came to Paris to consecrate him but Napoleon famously placed the imperial crown on his own head then crowned his wife. His European campaigns won him and his family numerous other crowns until he overstretched himself by trying to conquer Moscow. Napoleon abdicated in 1814.

Monarchy was restored and the exiled brother of the executed Louis XVI came back from England determined to go back to old royalist ways as if nothing had happened, even changing the tricolour flag back to white! He styled himself Louis XVIII to honour the memory of the missing *dauphin*, presumed executed like his father and mother Marie-Antoinette, although at least forty-three 'false dauphins' have come forward, claiming to have escaped from prison in various ways.

The first Restoration did not last long as Bonaparte staged a coup and was welcomed back in France. European allies could not tolerate their old enemy once more in power and the battle of Waterloo in 1815 sealed the end of the epic 'Hundred Days'. Napoleon was then exiled to the island of St Helena, after abdicating in favour of his son, another unhappy dauphin who stayed with his mother at the Viennese Court and died of TB at the age of twenty-two.

RIOTS & REPUBLICS

Louis XVIII was brought back to an unhappy, divided France, now to be ruled by ultra conservatives. At his death in 1824, his younger brother became king under the name of Charles X. Trying to rule without Parliament, ignoring various reforms as well as being insensitive to the general feeling of people who had lived through the troubled period when he himself had been safely abroad, he caused riots, then fled leaving the kingdom to another royal Valois, who accepted parliamentary power and acknowledged the Tricolour. He was crowned as Louis-Philippe in 1830 but made enough mistakes to provoke more riots. He fled in 1848 when the Republic was proclaimed again.

The Second Republic lasted four years as Louis-Napoleon Bonaparte, nephew of Napoleo I, was elected as its President, only to become Emperor in 1852! '*Plus ça change. . .*

The Second Empire, with its many achievements, survived until 1870 when defeat in the Franco-Prussian war, followed by the civil war known as the 'Commune', shook France and left dangerous feelings in the national consciousness. The loss of the Rhineland area of Alsace and Lorraine to Germany fuelled the desire for revenge leading to WW1. The murderous repression of mainly star-ving Parisian craftsmen, who had taken part in a democratic protest against political decisions, divided a country already torn by deep divisions: Paris was considered as 'red' by a conservative countryside, and did not regain a Mayor until 1977.

The Third Republic became the longest lasting as it stretched until WW2 (1870-1940) when it was dissolved after the French defeat and the collaborationist French 'State' installed in Vichy under Marshal Petain took over.

LIBERATION & RENEWAL

After the Liberation in 1944, General de Gaulle, who had formed a government in exile in London and had headed the Resistance, led the provisional government which organized elections for the Fourth Republic. It lasted until 1958, when the last dirty war of decolonization in Algeria saw France on the verge of civil war. De Gaulle stepped in again and was elected head of the Fifth Republic, with a stronger constitution.

After 1968 and its 'Events', Pompidou became president; he is best remembered for his interest in modern architecture as shown by the 'Centre Pompidou'. After Pompidou's death in office, Giscard d'Estaing was elected (1974-81), then socialist Mitterrand who holds the record for longest presidency (two seven-year mandates). He died in 1996, having seen his former Prime Minister, Chirac, succeed him in 1995.

The Republic is now definitively established in France. 1989 saw splendid celebrations of its bicentenary. The latest celebration saw four million people toast the Millennium together in the longest picnic route ever devised, crossing France north-south for six hundred miles with four hundred miles of special tablecloth. What was particularly special was that no expensive monument was built and that it happened on 14 July, the National Day of the Republic, along the old Paris Meridian, one degree after the Greenwich Meridian.

3

So, Who Are the French?

Getting the facts right . . .

By now the reader will have some questions in mind. No single answer will be satisfactory since the French themselves disagree on who they are and what their values are. Coming from abroad, one is further faced with the clichés between nations projected onto individuals without even being aware of it. Both French and foreigners are at fault and any effort at mutual comprehension is worthwhile. I will therefore concentrate on French attitudes to foreigners. Remember that *l'Etranger* (the outsider)), by Camus is one of the most famous modern French novels.

THE FRANCE-ENGLAND RIVALRY

Old clichés die hard and France and England have had enough poisonous history between them to fill textbooks with one-sided arrogance: from the Hundred Years' War and Joan of Arc as enemy or saint, to Gare d'Austerlitz in Paris and Waterloo Station in London referring to Napoleon as a hero or a crushed dictator – depending on who you are.

A more recent example which might shed light on how the same event can be interpreted in painfully different ways is what the British have called 'the spirit of Dunkirk', a meaningless phrase in France. It should act as a warning to any visitors not to assume that their nation is gratefully remembered anywhere, even in allied countries.

The 1940 'miraculous' evacuation of over 300,000 troops by an amazing assortment of British boats from the Dunkirk area, which at the time was surrounded by German forces, evokes solidarity in the face of adversity for the British, but a cynical betrayal for the French who saw the British evacuated first, while some 40,000 French soldiers were left to the Germans.

THE OTHER SIDE OF THE COIN

On 1 June 2000, the sixtieth anniversary of Dunkirk was marked on BBC Radio 4 by a discussion amongst historians. It was fascinating to hear British self-celebration still going on, coupled with a total absence of reference to the French, who after all, were living and fighting in Dunkirk, and whose injured feelings might be known by now! *Plus ça change, plus c'est pareil!* Similarly, and without going into details, but with first-hand knowledge of particular incidents, it may come as a surprise to visitors from allied countries that not all French people who lived through the war and the Liberation have feelings of gratitude. Surprisingly, some were treated more humanely when prisoners of war in Germany than when 'liberated'.

Just as puzzling is the impression of being trapped in an unknown scenario which has nothing to do with one's behaviour or one's country's, but refers purely to an ongoing hidden conflict within French society. This happened recently to a young British sculptor who had been living in France for six years and was asked to submit designs for a monument commemorating the Resistance heroes who died in the local 'maquis'. Although the local council was enthusiastic about his winged 'Victoire', which would have been the largest figurative monument to the Resistance in France, the mayor refused permission to erect it as being 'Communist inspired and made of rubbish'.

Hal Wilson said that he had no idea that his sculpture would provoke such a political-historical storm. He had grown up thinking that the war was simple and that the good guys had won. 'Around here, things are not that simple.' Eventually, the sculpture was given a home nearby, on the territory of a left-wing mayor. The tensions are worse in the area because it lies near the town of Vichy, and some people still think that the pro-German government led by Pétain was Catholic unlike the godless fighters of the Resistance! Hal Wilson was re-opening wounds which have not healed sixty years after the event.

GUARDING 'FRENCHNESS'

Learned articles in French historical publications talk of anti-Americanism disappearing from French university circles whereas francophobia seems to be growing in American academe, and they retrace the various stages of delusion among each side concerning political, economic or intellectual interference or perception of interference. The de Gaulle era was particularly fertile, when the challenge for France was to obtain prosperity, consumer goods and technology with American help and yet retain its Frenchness.

By establishing a policy of independence from the USA, the resentment which used to be expressed graphically by graffiti of 'Yankees go home' daubed on walls bearing the standard 'Défense d'afficher' ('notices prohibited'), evaporated. A reassessment of the so-called colonization of France has taken place and it is to be hoped that American academics guilty of francophobia will also come to realize that the projection of what may only be internal disputes onto the international scene is rarely productive. A good game, maybe?

Safeguarding 'Frenchness'

There are always worries about safeguarding 'Frenchness'; in fact, visitors who keep coming to France because of that special *je ne sais quoi* in the air should approve of French worries, even if they take ridiculous forms.

Can French survive in the face of the worldwide supremacy of American computer technology? Most sites are in English and despite the thunderings of the French Academy and its feeble offers of French jargon, a look at a French computer magazine reveals a disconcerting gobbledegook making IT seem very ET!

A recent discussion that I had with a 'cadre' (executive) in a French oil company reveals how people adapt. He was happy to contrast his own 'Frenglish', commonly used in his firm, with the 'proper' French used in a rival firm. Unfortunately, it took the latter three times as many staff to perform similar tasks and so they were being taken over. He commented that he would have to brush up his proper French to negotiate restructuring measures in their headquarters. His first job was to go and eat an enormous banquet with lots of duck delicacies, to show he was one of them.

HAUTE COUTURE

If one now switches to the realm of *haute couture*, one may be forgiven for being perplexed. The Home News page of a British daily recently carried lengthy reports on 'Paris fashion'; the odd connection between home and Paris possibly being explained by the fact that two British designers, A. McQueen and J. Galliano, newly-appointed heads of Givenchy and Dior couture houses respectively, were showing their first collections. Talent knows no borders indeed if they triumph in Paris. One also learns, however, that 'Britons' French couture staff 'cut up rough' (i.e. were extremely dissatisfied) and disrupted catwalk shows with fliers explaining that 'they [McQueen and Galliano] are very inexperienced and do not realize the time it takes to produce proper work'.

This report of worries amongst the *petites mains* (little hands, or expert seamstresses) was soon followed by metaphorical custard pies flying between the top nobs themselves, with Yves Saint-Laurent just about recovering from the vulgarity of the young English invaders whilst they kindly suggest retirement to the golden oldie so obviously 'out of fashion'!

Oh, dear! Despite dire predictions that the end is nigh for *haute couture*, the new millennium may well prove to bring a revival in its fortunes, while the optimistic Anglo-Saxon press asserts that 'America and Italy may now be competing in the lucrative business of designer sportswear . . . – but only Paris has couture – the jewel in the crown – as well as a national heritage . . . .

Not many of us are going to be affected by the extinction or resurrection of Parisian *haute couture*, but it seems to function powerfully as a cultural icon linking something perceived as typically French and the rest of the world. Will it be saved by new foreign blood in the context of grinding globalization, with only 2,000 clients left worldwide compared with 200,000 in 1943?

The situation is suitably amusing and refers us to other convoluted attitudes which in turn divide French public opinion concerning its responses to foreign products and influences, ranging from Coca-cola, MacDonalds, Walt Disney films and theme parks to NATO and especially the English language. Several examples are given in different chapters.

If you are more into *prêt-à-porter* (ready-to-wear) than Haute Couture, you may have past or future experiences similar to Tessa, the very English heroine in *The Things We Do For Love*,[2] by the other warmly recommended author, Lisa Appigna-nesi. See below:

2. Harper Collins, 1999 Omnibus edition ISBN 0-261-672-261-4

Extract from: 'The Things we do For Love'

Tessa hailed a taxi and asked to be taken to Saint-Germain. . . She found a little hotel in the Rue du Dragon, amidst antique shops and boutiques which wafted perfume, and women like iridescent butter-flies. She sat in her hotel room. . . and felt like a faded moth waiting for the light. At last she forced herself to pick up the receiver and dial.

A clear, self-sufficient voice replied, eliciting messages with seductive charm. . . She couldn't face the owner of that voice. Not yet. In any event, what would she say?

No, a little more preparation was necessary. . . This different mirror, which she forced herself to look into, reflected a woman who was all but invisible, too pale, too thin, insignificant. All her fears were written large within its gilded frame. And it shouted at her, told her how much she had let herself go these last years, had become merely the woman who couldn't have a baby, not a sexed creature at all, really, just a shadow. . .

When she looked at herself, Tessa had to admit that she was pleased. . .

Tessa tipped him generously. She also followed his orders and promptly found a *parfumerie* where a woman advised her on blushers and bases and shadows and lipstick. She went further than that. At a boutique near the salon, she bought herself a beautifully tailored jacket in a rich charcoal-brown, a matching skirt, shorter than anything she had worn for years, striped trousers with loose pleats at the top and pencil slim at the base, and two jerseys recommended by the assistant, who was as quick to point out what didn't suit her as what did.

She wanted nothing more than to be made over. In the morning the courage of make-up almost failed her, but she chivvied herself along the Boulevard Saint-Germain into the narrow streets of the fifth arrondissement. . .

So why does *The Independent* for example (8/5/2000) enjoy publishing an article with the big headline: **Why are the British the stuff of French nightmares?** Napoleon was apparently poisoned by the British on his island prison of St Helena, the French Senate has just heard! Not content with complaining about a 100-year-old presumed crime by Britain, they also seethe about 'le king Tony' trying to take over the EU pushing the British policy of a large free-trade area without commitment to integration, at a time when Franco-German relations are not as warm as they have been.

This shows that the fascination is ongoing, despite its negative presentation. Happy stories do not make for interesting journalism any more than novels. In the novel quoted above, but on the page before sending her heroine to Paris, Appignanesi has her reminisce about her English family and the myth of Britishness:

> On impulse last year Tessa had sent her father a book she had edited. It contended that Britishness was an eighteenth-century invention, not some primordial essence. The invention had taken shape over what could be seen as a hundred years' war with the French. It was a useful invention, since it kept England and Scotland and Wales united against the enemy. One of its wheels was the Bank of England. Another was the propaganda, which became assumed fact, labelling the nasty, foppish French everything the brave and manly, sincere and innocent British were not: Catholic, superstitious, militaristic, wasteful, corrupt, oppressed, badly paid and self-flaunting, garlic eating hypocrites to boot. So being British had only taken on meaning when set against the French, our closest and preferred enemy. The problem was that now that we are all supposed to be friends in one not altogether comfortable union, the very idea of Britishness teetered precariously, no longer able to gloss over a spectrum of internal differences.
>
> But her father was impervious to rational argument. He clung to his prejudices, as much a part of him as his digestive tract.

Hot Tip: Follow your Host's Lead

General advice as far as foreign visitors are concerned would be to observe and carefully notice what their French neighbours are doing; watch them, imitate them and praise them. Then, once conversation is going in a friendly way ask them for their opinions on different issues.

'ENTENTE CORDIALE'

The 'entente cordiale' is, however, fortunately a phrase common to both British and French language and culture and with us to stay. It did not come about easily, but King Edward VII, *'le roi charmeur'*, conquered the anglophobia of the French with his personal touch at the turn of the twentieth century. Even popular songs begrudgingly admitted he was welcome in France since:

> *Quand il n'était que prince /*
> *De son sale pays [..] / Il venait à Paris [..] /*
> *Et ne quittait la table / Que huit jours après!*

('When he was but a Prince in his rotten country, he came to Paris and only left the table a week later.') As a return gesture, the French President was feted in London and treated to a chorus of British and French sailors on the stage, whilst a French and an English comedienne dressed respectively as Marianne and Britannia, joined hands to sing together the National anthem and *La Marseillaise*, a feat no military endeavour had ever achieved.

THE OTHER FACES OF FRANCE

As a contrast to Paris, with all its historic images of romance, style and singular prowess, it is necessary to introduce an enduring aspect of French life which makes sense to foreign visitors because the French believe in it so strongly themselves: this is the countryside, or Deep France, (*'la France profonde'*) which commands such an attachment.

It is unfortunately true to say that there is also another 'face' of France, which bears the mask of racism.

The National Front is now in disarray, however, due to internecine quarrelling. Nevertheless, better safe than sorry. It is regrettable to have to advise visitors to France that if they are young and non-white, they have to be especially careful to carry their identity papers at all times (passport and driving licence). This is precisely because they are likely to be treated like the local population, and might come across cases of police racism. They are more likely to be stopped and searched especially in tube stations such as *Châtelet / Les Halles* where a lot of pickpockets operate.

It is better to look like a tourist; try and protest in French: *Je suis américain/australien/britannique. Je me plaindrai/je protesterai au service diplomatique/à l'ambassade/au consulat.* (I am American/Australian/British. I shall complain/protest to the diplomatic services/the embassy/the consulate). Make sure you practise in your hotel room before venturing out, just for fun, and hope you never need it.

This is not to say that you will not find courteous police ready to help you on your way. Take for instance the memorable scene in Kassowitz's film *La Haine* in which three young friends of varied ethnic groups from a poor housing estate in the Parisian suburbs where conflict between police and youth is endemic, come to central Paris and experience police politeness. They cannot believe that they have been called 'Monsieur' and given directions. The fact that they were actually trying to find the posh flat of their drug dealer adds further irony!

The last World Cup took place in Paris in 1998, in *Le Grand Stade* which is now the latest tourist site for those interested in football. France won it with a team composed of players of every hue drawn mainly from non Franco-French ethnic backgrounds. As a result attitudes have become more positive towards minorities. That a sporting victory became an anti-racist victory demonstrated the power available to France if its different elements work in harmony.

AVOID TROUBLE

Whatever your colour/age/religion ... avoid any demo(nstration) *manif(estation)* unless of course it is your reason for coming to France and you know what you are doing. You might find yourself in the wrong crowd beaten up for the wrong cause! The procession in honour of Joan of Arc on 1 May has little to do with religion and a lot with fascist elements testing their strength. So find a first-floor window in a café if you must watch, and hope for the best.

While on the topic of reactions to minorities, it is here assumed that anyone visiting France with a problem of mobility, for instance, will have made enquiries before setting off regarding access to the museums, hotels, and public transport. More local information is available from local Tourist Offices.

People wishing to meet French gays will have their own network or will find it easier to access information and clubs while in Paris before venturing further afield. French laws have become egalitarian in their treatment of same-sex partners and reductions for couples on the French Railways apply equally. Discretion in street behaviour is however preferred.

POST-COLONIAL TRAUMA

You will have gathered that France has not yet come to terms with the trauma of decolonisation, the influx of immigrants from Black Africa and especially North Africa (called the Maghreb). The second-generation of North-African origin are often called 'Beur', a word they used to pun on their Arab identity. They have now developed a vibrant youth culture and people sometimes speak of the new Tricolour being 'black, blanc, beur'.

Yet, France is also at the same time actively pursuing policies designed to consolidate a French-speaking commonwealth, 'la Francophonie'. Recent summits have taken place as far away as Hanoi. It is a political as well as a cultural club. Hence some countries where French used to be well-known have refused to join because independence has meant arabization, whereas others see French as a cultural tool well worth preserving despite the colonial past. Louisiana is part of it, Quebec too, and Belgium and Switzerland; also, many West African countries, the West Indies, Vietnam and Cambodia.

Despite this official attitude, Francophone Studies are more seriously pursued in US and UK universities than in French ones, and a writer of the stature of Assia Djebar, an Algerian writing in French, is recognized and celebrated everywhere (Neuschtad prize for world literature 1996, USA) but hardly in France.

Some say that Europe is the privileged partner and that 'la Francophonie' is second best. There is no longer any great enthusiasm, yet steadily, the French have embraced the idea of Europe and are working towards it. The Franco-German cultural TV channel 'Arte' is surprisingly popular in unexpected quarters as its coverage of current affairs is seen as more neutral than national channels.

A February 1997 cover of *Le Nouvel Observateur*, a well-known French weekly, graphically shows how French society is struggling not to let its century-old reputation of being a fraternal land of freedom open to newcomers be sullied. It featured a 'Stop' roadsign with the legend 'NO TO RACIST FRANCE'. For whether the majority of the people realize it or not, the population of present-day France contains one-third of inhabitants who were foreigners one, two or three generations ago, making France the largest melting-pot in Europe.

If we now turn away from how the French behave towards others to what they cherish for themselves. I would emphasize culture. Culture is revered. A philosopher was asked to write a thirteen-page essay for the French edition of *Playboy*. Intelligence is seen as sexy and French films exploring this fascination abound. There is a Ministry for Culture. Jack Lang, who acquired popular fame there under a former government, is still one of the most liked and trusted politicians in France.

Hot Tip: France Loves Intellectuals

It is an honour, not an embarrassment to be labelled an 'intellectual' and Paris has not been the capital of artists and writers for nothing; James Joyce and Henry James were at home there to mention but two famous names.

Sophistication and seduction go together; try Appignanesi's sexy novels and Zeldin's erudition on 'amitié amoureuse' (loving friendship) (p.329) where we learn of the Marquise de Lambert concluding that 'the heart needed to be educated, just as the brain was, and that affection could be studied as a work of art'.

So try and take in one of the many festivals going on throughout the year, for music, theatre, dance or film. Cinema is taken very seriously as the Seventh Art. Paris is of course the prime place to see old films from all over the world which can be found only with difficulty in archives elsewhere, hence the love-hate relationship with Hollywood productions.

Jazz is very popular, and some more recent music from (North) Africa is also gaining ground. There are interesting mixtures of old French poetry put to Arab music. Lyrics are traditionally important in a French 'chanson' as the enduring popularity of Piaf, Brel and Brassens shows.

Architecture on the grand scale is an ongoing concern and French Presidents have taken over from the kings as far as prestigious buildings in Paris are concerned. The same is true on a smaller scale in the provinces.

Besides culture, I might select health. According to a recent survey, health matters more than family life or career or 'amour' in making a person happy. Watching from abroad, I call them hypochondriacs and pack paracetamol with me to save visits to doctors. See 'Facts' for more details.

So pick and choose your own feelings and attitudes to France. You are following in the path of many others who have enjoyed the idiomatic ways of the natives for a multitude of reasons. All of them have found it, if not always a cosy experience, at least a worthwhile challenge.

Hot Tip: An Old Saying. . .

Remember the old saying that every civilized person has two countries: their own and France. Your genuine liking for or desire to like France will be warmly appreciated.

4

Meeting People

Winter sport

People shake hands when they meet and before parting again. It is usual for the senior person to proffer his or her hand first. If you enter a room where there are several people, shake hands with everyone; failing to shake hands might be interpreted as a sign of hostility, so it is important not to forget the handshake.

When you greet people, the proper way is to say: *'Bonjour monsieur'* to a man, *'Bonjour, madame'* to a woman, *'Bonjour, mademoiselle'* to a young lady.

French children are drilled to learn the polite formulae; always adding *madame, mademoi-*

selle, monsieur after **all** greetings (not just *Bonjour*, but *Au revoir* (Goodbye) and *Bonsoir* (Good evening); *Pardon* is very useful before asking for directions or the time. Keep *'Salut!'* (Hi!) to greet **back** a well-known person who first uses this familiar expression.

The French tend to be rather formal and do not use first names easily. They might be friends and still address each other with *'Monsieur X'* or *'Madame Y'*. Things are changing with the younger generation, but to be on the safe side, never use the first name unless you have been expressly asked to do so; otherwise, it might be resented as being too familiar.

French people have two ways of addressing each other: the formal *vous*; or the more familiar *tu*, which is reserved for their family and close friends – or even colleagues in certain circles.

Hot Tip: How to Address your Mother-in-law

Even the French hesitate between *tu* and *vous*. How do you address your mother-in-law? It is for the most senior person to suggest a switch to *tu*. If your mother-in-law does not, then you are stuck with *vous* for the next half-century or so.

Conversely, young or more junior people who are invited to use *tu* may find it quite difficult. People of the same age or similar background coming together for the first time may also be unsure of the right form to use. It will be fun for you to listen to conversations and notice what is going on around you.

Hot Tip: Avoid Familiarity in Business

You might call a colleague of yours who is a friend by his first name and address him with *tu* when you are at home or alone, but you may have to revert to *madame/monsieur* and *vous* when you are back at work and in official meetings. The French tend not to mix their private life with the world of work.

Instead of shaking hands, relatives and close friends kiss each other (two, three or four times depending on the region where you are staying). Once again, take heart: most French people have been left with one cheek in the air because they expected to receive a further kiss. Everyone is happy to laugh together! Kisses are also conveyed in correspondence: *Grosses bises, gros baisers, Je vous embrasse,* are all simply equivalent of the English *Love* (all equally shocking because out of place if taken literally!)

WRITING LETTERS

The reverse does, however, also happen in letters: the two coded British formulae *Yours sincerely* and *Yours faithfully* are woefully inadequate when compared with the time-honoured French formal endings which take such an effort to master and so long to write, but are a real feather in your cap once you have remembered them:

> *Veuillez agréer, Madame/Monsieur/ Mademoiselle, l'expression de mes sentiments dévoués/les meilleurs*

As you may guess, your choice should match the person addressed at the top of the letter as *Madame*, or other. You will **not** have included *Cher* or *Chère* in front of *Monsieur* or *Madame* as this would be judged too familiar. The French may live in a republic but some forms of polite social etiquette do smack of courtly protocol.

CONVERSATIONAL TECHNIQUES

Compared to Northern Europeans, French people are extrovert; their conversation is often reinforced by gestures. When taking part in a discussion in a group, they do not wait until someone has finished making a point, they interrupt and put forward their own ideas. This is not considered impolite; quick exchanges are the rule. If the discussion gets heated, the person who speaks or shouts loudest seems to win the argument. To an outsider this might appear aggressive, but not in the eyes of the French, who are brought up to be competitive.

Conversation is frequently peppered with witty remarks. The French have a satirical sense of humour — but at other people's expense. If someone makes fun of them, they are touchy or even hurt; they consider it rude and defend themselves in an unexpectedly forceful manner.

HOME & FAMILY LIFE

It is said that foreigners, although they find French people friendly enough, are disappointed because they are not readily invited into French homes. The reason is that the French only want the best for their guests; everything has to be perfect, especially the food. Lunch or dinner offered to guests will invariably require considerable preparation which is one reason why a formal invitation may not happen straight away. But when it comes, it is a very special treat indeed. Be prepared to spend several hours at the dining table; for the French, a meal is the ideal social occasion, involving plenty of eating, drinking and talking.

French people are individualistic, insisting on doing things their own way even if it means bending the rules; but at the same time they seldom rebel against the constraints of family life. When they do, it is fairly traumatic. Many a novel refers to the tensions involved.

Youngsters tend to stay at home much longer than their Northern European counterparts. Even when they start working, it is not unusual for them to stay with their parents until they marry. If they enter higher education, they attend the university nearest to their home. Children remain close to their grandparents, uncles, aunts and cousins.

Sunday lunch, whether at home or in a restaurant, is invariably a family affair often including relatives living in the same district. This is especially the case in the provinces where families are not as scattered.

French people are generally reluctant to move from one region to another even if job prospects are better; the only exception is moving from the provinces to Paris. The aim of most people's career seems to be to become senior enough to be able to choose being posted **back** to their native regions.

STATE & RELIGION

Traditionally France is a Catholic country but in recent times the church has lost a great deal of its influence. Although many people might not be church-goers, they still celebrate religious festivals which punctuate the different stages of life: birth, adolescence and marriage. *Baptême* for babies, *communion solennelle* for twelve-year-olds, and weddings, are occasions for big family gatherings with huge meals lasting several hours.

The French seem to have devised ways of putting Religion and State on a par so that everyone is happy. This is shown in their main festivals, at winter and summer-time. Christmas and New Year are celebrated very much in the same way, with

'Vive la France'

similar meals at odd times called by the same name (*réveillon*). The storming of the old prison of the Bastille in Paris is the event celebrated as the Republic's founding date on 14 July, with days off, dancing and fireworks. One month later, on 15 August, the same type of celebrations occur but this time for the Assumption, which few people realize is the Roman Catholic festival of the raising to heaven of the Virgin Mary.

With the arrival of many North African immigrants, Islam has become the second most important religion in France. There is also a Protestant minority which plays a fairly important role, despite being small in number; many of its members occupy leading positions in politics or the civil service. The population also includes a Jewish community, influential in trade and the media. (For details of these religions, see the World Religions series of Simple Guides, especially Islam.)

Hot Tip: Understand the Key Word Laïcité

The key word here is *LAICITE* (=laïcité): it basically means that France as a state is neutral in matters of belief, refusing to privilege one above the other, but allowing free worship or atheism as personal choices. It does not mean that atheism is the doctrine of the State as in the former Communist block. It means freedom and equality for all citizens when the laws work well.

Laïcité is welcomed by minorities who were oppressed in the past by the Roman Catholic Church when it was the official religion and France was 'the eldest daughter of the Church'. Restorations of the monarchy tended to be Catholic-led and the Republic was only established with difficulty. Hence the occasional worries of French citizens when they see outward displays of religion.

The effective separation of Church and State only dates from 1905, although a formula had been found earlier with the system of the 'Concordat' negotiated by Napoleon in 1801.

Because Alsace and Lorraine were part of Germany in 1905, they still have this historical agreement as law. Hence Strasbourg is the only university with a theology department. In fact, two corridors have been allocated, one to Protestants, who are strong in the region, and one to Catholic theologians. The region is also the only one to pay rabbis, pastors and priests the same salary as a schoolteacher!

Elsewhere, religion is forbidden in state schools although some now say that a course in history or philosophy of religion might be a good idea to understand the social and cultural diversity and encourage enlightened tolerance, but resistance is strong for fear of proselytizing.

LANGUAGES & TRAVEL

In France, the older generation are not very good at speaking other languages. Foreign language teaching used to be very formal, based on learning grammar and the study of literary texts and not aimed at communicating effectively with foreigners. French was the language spoken by diplomats and educated foreigners visiting France. French people were not really keen on travelling and living abroad except perhaps in the French colonies; they were so confident in the superiority of everything French that they did not feel any need to communicate in another language.

Now attitudes and teaching methods have changed a great deal. Foreign language learning is encouraged at an early age, even at kindergarten and primary school. In many business schools English is compulsory and work experience abroad is highly valued.

Hot Tip: The French may Reply in English!

Do not be upset if your attempts at communicating in French are thwarted by people talking back to you in English. It is mostly the case that they want to practise their skills and also make you feel at ease.

The best preparation for conversational French is to use cassettes as well as phrase-books because pronunciation is based on vowel sounds and not on consonants which are very often unvoiced at the end of words unless they precede a word starting with a vowel, producing the famous *liaison*, e.g., 'comment allez-vous?' There are no stressed syllables. All this means that words like 'telephone' or 'table' which are written in the same way in French and English do sound quite different. (See pp.85/86.)

5

French Homes

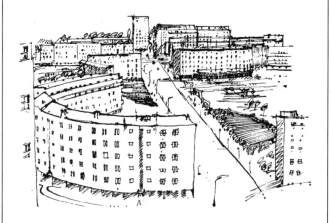

Modern apartment blocks near Paris

Rented apartments rather than private houses are the norm in French towns and cities. The entrance to each apartment block used to be watched by the *concierge* or *gardien* who was in charge of distributing the mail and keeping the staircases clean, but in modern buildings you have to press the intercommunication button of the person you want to visit, state your name and he or she will open the main entrance by remote control. Individual doors are fitted with a brass plaque or a card carrying the name of the occupant.

If you do not see any such communication devices, you may be stuck a long time outside the *porte cochère*, or former carriage entrance, especially with old buildings in Paris. So here is the 'sesame' formula: Is there a button to press? Then do so but although there will be a buzzing noise, do not expect any answer; it is the signal for you to push the door open. During the day, it will probably be enough to get in. Once inside the communal corridor, you may find a grill barring your (and the tramps') way. At this stage, you will have access to the interphone and the letter boxes.

At night or for all sorts of reasons, you may find that pressing the button and leaning on the door will serve no purpose: you can only enter if you have been given the secret code to tap on the pad next to the button. If you have been invited and cannot get in, the only solution is to telephone from the nearest booth or café. The first time can be extremely frustrating; then you learn to ask for the code and to jot it down for the next visit.

The dream of every Frenchman is to have his own house built to his own specifications. On new housing estates you will find a great variety of houses surrounded by a clearly delimited garden. However, in order not to spoil the character of an area, regulations put a curb on the individuality and creativity of French builders. Houses have to be in keeping with the traditional buildings of the region. For example, in Brittany where roofs are

'The dream of every Frenchman . . .'

covered with slates, it is prohibited to use tiles which are traditionally used in the South.

Many town-dwellers have a second home. Because of the exodus from rural areas, increasing numbers of village houses and farm buildings are deserted and bought as *résidences secondaires* where city-dwellers spend their week-ends and holidays. You do not have to be very rich to afford these properties, except in the most sought-after areas in the South, on the Riviera for instance, where prices are high.

Hot Tip: Keep Out of the Kitchen!

If you are invited into a French home, remember that the kitchen may be a no-go area. Do not insist on helping to carry things from the table or doing the washing-up; you would only embarrass your host or hostess who would probably think you were being nosy.

6

Eating & Drinking

Le petit déjeuner – breakfast

Two cooked meals a day – lunch and an evening meal – are usually eaten in France. For breakfast, coffee is drunk (often with milk) out of a bowl rather than a cup; children drink either white coffee or chocolate. White crispy bread is spread with butter and jam. Figure-conscious people eat *biscotte*, a kind of toasted bread. On Sundays, the first one up buys freshly baked *croissants*.

Lunch-time usually lasts for two hours and whenever possible the whole family comes together. As schoolchildren start work at 8.30 am and finish at 4.30 pm or later, schools provide a canteen to cater for those who cannot go home.

Lunch usually consists of a main course which might be meat or fish and vegetables, preceded by a starter and followed by lettuce, cheese and/or a dessert. There is always a basket of bread on the table as French people eat bread throughout the meal, **except** with soup. However tempting fresh, crispy bread might be, refrain from nibbling at a piece before the meal actually starts

'People linger at table'

Hot Tip: Don't Wipe the Plate Clean!

Always break the bread with your fingers, never cut it. There are no side plates for bread, so do not worry if crumbs go all over the table. It is often assumed that the French use bread to clean their plates. Although they might occasionally indulge in this practice privately at home in order to eat a particularly delicious sauce, doing it in the presence of guests is considered bad manners.

or between courses, or your host will think you are desperately hungry.

As usual, the golden rule is to watch the natives, and do the same. The one rule of politeness you should try consciously to observe concerns the position of your hands when you eat. Because the rule, just like driving on the right on the other side of the Channel, is the exact opposite of the English one, it may produce unease at first. The sacred rule is to keep your left hand and wrist (not the elbow!) **on** the table during the meal, **not under**.

When children return from school, they have a *goûter* which consists of a piece of bread with a bar of chocolate or a pastry and a bowl of *café au lait* or *chocolat au lait*.

Most people finish work at 6.00 pm, consequently the evening meal does not start until 7.00 or 8.00 pm. The whole family gathers around the dining-table, even young children, and might well listen to or watch the news broadcast.

On Sundays, more members of the extended family may be reunited and meals are more elaborate. They are preceded by an *apéritif*, a drink like Martini or other fortified wines including *porto* (port), whisky, which is cheaper in France, and various brand names are discussed by enthusiastic connoisseurs, a typically French *pastis* (a drink flavoured with aniseed) or *Suze* (a bitter drink made with herbs).

Starters consist of salads, *charcuterie* (cold sliced meat and sausages) or shellfish. A special meal might have two main courses. Vegetables are sometimes served on their own after the main course. Refrain from using the salt and pepper cellars even if they are on the table; adding more spices would imply that the person who prepared the meal did not get it right. To refresh the palate lettuce tossed in oil and vinegar is served, followed by cheese. The meal ends with the dessert: cake or ice-cream for example, and fruit.

The *boulangerie* – bread for all tastes

People linger at the table, drink coffee and *digestifs* such as Cognac, Calvados (apple brandy) or *liqueurs*: Cointreau or Grand Marnier (orange-based), Chartreuse or Bénédictine (made with herbs). If you are a smoker, this is when you might light a cigarette. It would be very rude to smoke during the meal as it prevents you and others from properly tasting and appreciating the food the hostess has spent hours preparing.

WINE

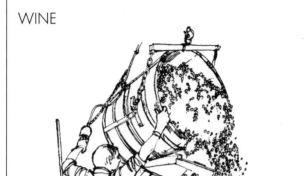

Wine-making: delivering grapes into the press

Wine is the traditional drink. If it is ordinary table wine, it might be diluted with water to quench the thirst but if it is good quality wine, it is drunk straight in little sips. As soon as your glass is empty, it will be replenished; if you do not want to drink a lot, always leave something in your glass.

Although tap water is all right, French people insist on drinking bottled water. In a restaurant if you want to avoid the expense of mineral water (which can be very pricey) ask for *une carafe d'eau*, tap water which is provided free.

Hot Tip: The Secret of Choosing Wine

Drinking and enjoying wine is an art. For the experience to be perfect, wine has to have the right colour, smell and taste, and be at the right temperature. It is chosen to match the taste of the food of the different courses. This is why you should not bring a bottle of wine if you are invited because you will not know the menu. Champagne, however, is a possibility as is a quality spirit.

Different wines are served during the meal: *rosé* or *blanc sec* (dry white) with starters, *rouge* (red) with meat, dry white with fish, *blanc doux* (sweet white) with the dessert. Before drinking wipe your lips with your napkin and hold your glass by the stem in order not to leave marks on the glass which would prevent you from fully appreciating the colour and quality of the wine.

REGIONAL CUISINE & SPECIAL DISHES

The pattern of a French meal always remains the same, but the content can vary tremendously depending on the area. Due to its varied geography and climate, France has a great range of products which are used in rich and original regional cuisines. Normandy is famous for its specialities cooked in cream and apple brandy, Brittany for its seafood, Burgundy for dishes cooked in wine, Périgord for poultry preserved in its own fat (*confit de canard* or *d'oie*) and dishes flavoured with truffles.

If you are treated to '*foie gras*', do not insult your hosts by thinking it is mere *pâté*. Provence will offer dishes including olive oil, garlic, tomatoes and peppers. Northern areas use butter and onions, southern areas oil and garlic in their cooking. Although wine is drunk everywhere in France, cider is the traditional drink in the West and beer in the East and extreme North.

Important events of a private nature are celebrated with a special meal. Christmas and New Year, of course, are also occasions for a big meal: *le réveillon*. Traditionally, oysters, which are at their best at this time of the year, are served as starters, followed by a special choice of *charcuterie* which might well include *foie gras* (goose or duck liver preserved in its own fat). The main course is goose, capon or turkey served with chestnuts, followed by lettuce, a choice of cheeses and a cake shaped like a log. The *réveillon* takes place on Christmas Eve, and gifts are also exchanged between members of the family.

New Year's Eve is a similar occasion often celebrated with friends rather than relatives. It is called *la Saint-Sylvestre* because of the name of the saint remembered on that day in yesteryears. Greetings are exchanged at midnight and Champagne is drunk to toast the New Year. If you are in Paris, take your bottle and join the crowds milling on the Champs-Elysées, as traffic is banned for the night: it is a wonderful sight with all the Christmas decorations and floodlit monuments; but here is a word of caution concerning making your way back. Either be sure that you **do** know the time of the last metro train or be ready to foot it as taxis will have been booked long in advance.

French people are immensely proud of their cooking and wine; they are convinced that nothing is better. Even if your grasp of French is limited, be sure you show your appreciation of a meal by your facial expression – or by taking second helpings! Then you will be regarded as good company and worth inviting again. How about learning: *'Madame, votre cuisine est magnifique!'*

Be ready to taste new food; declining to sample a dish prepared by your host would be very rude. If you can speak some French, do not hesitate to ask questions about the food being served; besides consuming food, talking about it is a favourite French pastime. In so doing, your reputation will be greatly enhanced and you will be respected as a foreigner who understands what really matters.

Hot Tip: Be a Good Guest!

If you are invited for a meal, arrive promptly; the different stages will have been carefully timed, so do not put all the efforts of the cook at risk by arriving late.

It is customary to present flowers to the hostess, but not chrysanthemums which in France are associated with death (they are put on graves on 1 November). Choose an odd number of flowers but avoid 13. A box of chocolates is also a traditional gift. **Remember that a bottle of wine is not a good idea.**

A meal is not just about food – conversation is almost as important. In a festive meal which can last several hours, there is plenty of time for discussion between courses. Although no topic is really taboo, talking about money is not welcome; asking a person how much he/she earns or what has been paid for a certain item would cause embarrassment.

THE RIGHT TOPICS FOR CONVERSATION

It goes without saying, of course, that certain topics are best avoided unless you are in a position to understand the language well, feel that you are on sympathetic wave-lengths and have some historical knowledge of events you may genuinely be interested to hear about from witnesses of the period; the Second World War is still a difficult subject for some – remember the saga of the British sculptor in Auvergne mentioned earlier. Much more so is the Algerian War and the sequels of decolonization and racism. You may, however, remember that most topics are touched upon with seemingly vindictive ardour at the end of the meal, *entre la poire et le fromage*, (between pear and cheese – a strange expression since fruit is always served after cheese) and yet with no hard feelings. It may just be a way of prolonging the twin pleasures of food and conversation.

Meals are treated seriously, even when matters of life and death are at stake. Fascinating details, for example, are known concerning Louis XVI's last meals before he ascended the scaffold in

1793: according to Franklin, he had three soups, four entrées, three roast dishes, four sweet courses, fancy cakes, three compotes, three fruit dishes, Champagne, Bordeaux, Malvoisie, and Madeira wines followed by coffee!

In January 1996, President Mitterand died of cancer. From the many biographies published, one learns of his last painful days; for the *réveillon* of *la Saint-Sylvestre* at his country house, although unable to sit at the table, he insisted on the traditional fare with his family and close friends and ate even more than them, downing three dozen oysters, two ortolans as well as *foie gras* and capon. Then he went back to Paris alone with his doctor; there he refused to touch food again and died a few days later.

WHERE TO EAT AND DRINK

A great range of restaurants can be found throughout France. You do not have to spend a lot of money to obtain a good meal. To a certain extent, the prices can reflect the quality of service rather than that of the food provided. For example, in the lower price range, the cutlery probably will not be changed with every course. The menu and prices are displayed outside restaurants.

Hot Tip: How to Order Steak

It is worth trying smaller places specializing in regional cooking but if you are in a hurry, do as the French do and order a *steak frites* (steak and chips).

When ordering steak, keep in mind that to a French cook *saignant* (rare) means the steak is just sealed on both sides. If you like your meat pink ask for *à point* or *bien cuit* if you cannot face under-cooked meat.

Often it is better value to choose a *menu* (set menu) rather than *à la carte*. A set menu might include wine, whereas a very reasonably-priced meal can become much more expensive when you order wine separately as restaurateurs make most of their profits on drinks. If you are not sure which wine would be appropriate for a particular dish, ask for advice - the restaurateur will take pride in choosing the right wine for you. If you decided to order something completely unsuitable, such as red wine with fish, for example, he probably would not be able to resist putting you right straight away.

If you are travelling and want to stop for a meal on the main road, *Routiers* restaurants are to be recommended. They cater mainly (but not exclusively) for long-distance drivers, providing good and very substantial meals at a reasonable price; the longer the queue of articulated lorries in the car park, the better the food is likely to be.

*B*rasseries also provide meals but the choice of dishes is not as great as in restaurants. You are expected to order a full meal in a restaurant but in a brasserie ordering just the main course is fine.

A Routiers restaurant

*C*rêperies are places which specialize in pancakes, sweet 'crêpes' and savoury 'galettes'. In Brittany and Normandy, the pancakes are accompanied by delicious sparkling cider served in bowls.

*C*afés are convivial places where friends meet, chat and watch the world go by. They are open from early morning until late at night, serving not only coffee but also alcoholic and soft drinks; one favourite is *citron pressé*, freshly squeezed lemon juice with water, ice-cubes and sugar to taste served in a large glass.

Hot Tip: Price of a Drink = Where you Sit!

The price for one drink may be thought to be extortionate, and it is, especially in some areas of Paris or on the main squares in the provinces. This is because you are buying the right to sit there, idling on their terrace.

Remember that if you decide to sit inside or outside on the terrace, drinks will be more expensive than when you stand at the counter. Service is by law now included in the price, but the waiter may still expect a tip (*pourboire*).

Cafés also prepare snacks: sandwiches with *jambon* (ham), *saucisson* (salami), *rillette* (pork spread), *fromage* (cheese) or a hot *croque monsieur*, a ham and cheese toasted sandwich.

Cafés-Tabac, which display a red carrot-shaped sign outside, not only sell tobacco but also sell stamps, phonecards and, in Paris, Metro/bus tickets.

Do not worry unduly about eating etiquette; follow the normal rule, watch (discreetly) your neighbours and imitate. It all depends on where you are. You might be greeted as old friends and your kids taken to see the pet rabbits in a village café-bar in the back of beyond while you are served the most delicious home-made stew. On the other hand, the butler may sneer down his nose at your lack of *savoir-faire* if you do not handle your ten instruments to crack, pinch, squeeze, eviscerate and somehow retrieve some substance out of your platter of 'fruits de mer' in an upmarket fish restaurant with maximum elegance. Having survived the ordeal, I now find it amusing. But if it is not for you, keep to steak.

The only recommendation would be to observe the non-smoking areas and be sensitive to your non-smoking neighbours. If they are not to you, ask the *garçon* to help. Keep you voice as low as the general level. Do not annoy the next table by insisting on treating your boyfriend or girlfriend to a narrative on the history of the world or the intricacies of Picasso and Braque in a loud American accent. They might be courting their sweetheart more seductively in softer tones.

7

Business Contacts

La Defense, Paris – centre for trade, business and industry

French business people, especially the older generation, behave very formally. You are expected to dress smartly, shake hands with everybody, address individuals with the formal *vous* and use titles correctly. More and more young people speak English. Women are increasingly represented at management level in certain industries, particularly in Paris.

In French companies the managing director (*PDG – Président Directeur Général*) exercises control to an extent that some foreigners may find surprising. His authority is based on competence; he takes all the important decisions himself and his attitude to his subordinates is aloof.

If you wish to contact senior executives, do not rely too much on their 'secretary', who does not usually have the authority to make appointments.

Sometimes, it may be difficult to organize meetings because French executives tend not to commit themselves until the last moment. Punctuality is expected of you, but you might have to wait if another engagement is considered more important than yours. Business appointments can be made during office hours, usually from 9.00 am to 6.00 pm. Some business people do not like to start the day in a hurry and will not see people before 9.30 am or even later, although you may be given a late appointment after 6.00 pm. In the world of show business do not expect anything to happen before 11.30 am.

When drawing up contracts, the French side will insist on precision; a verbal agreement is only a preliminary to a written agreement, which alone is legally binding. As long as written documents have not been signed, you cannot be sure of having secured anything.

Hot Tip: Pay the Bill & be Precise!

Business is still often done over an elaborate meal or perhaps during coffee at the end of it. The person who is trying to secure a contract pays for the meal.

During negotiations you are expected to be clear, consistent and precise; things have to be logical to be accepted. French people appreciate abstract discussion and projects which are well thought out but do not care much about pragmatism.

Most people take their holidays in August, and this month is therefore best avoided as far as promoting business is concerned.

The French style of letter-writing is extremely formal. Do not be surprised if after a friendly meeting you receive a letter written in convoluted language. The French are notorious for taking a long time in answering letters – if you do need a prompt answer send a fax or telephone.

e-mail is officially *'courrier électronique'* (now 'courriel' for short) but also called 'le mel' in office parlance. The web is its official *'la toile'* but most often *'le web'*. Different companies develop their own culture around the idiomatic use of French. So depending on whom you are negotiating with, a smile of connivance or apology can accompany your own Frenglish.

8

Travelling Around

TGV – Train à Grande Vitesse

DRIVING

If you drive in France, remember the following speed limits:

130 kph (80 mph) on **motorways**

90 kph (55 mph) on **other roads**

50 kph (30 mph) in **built-up areas**

Not all French drivers observe these limits, but if they are caught speeding, there are on-the-spot fines. A solidarity has developed among drivers and if you see a vehicle coming in the opposite direction flashing its headlights, it is a warning that *gendarmes* (policemen) are not far away, and for a few miles motorists will adjust their speed and behave as exemplary drivers.

Furthermore, French drivers tend not to be too considerate towards pedestrians – even at pedestrian crossings. In order to remedy this, speed ramps are being introduced. They are made so high that it would ruin the suspension of your car if you were to drive over them at more than 20 kph. At last pedestrians in France have a chance to cross the roads with some degree of safety!

As a rule, you have to give way to traffic coming from the right, even if you are on a main road. Roundabouts are becoming more numerous but there seem to be no uniform rules as to who has right of way. When you arrive at a roundabout, a sign will advise you if you can proceed or not; *Cédez le passage* or *Vous n'avez pas la priorité* indicates you have to give way to traffic already on the roundabout.

Except for short sections around towns, French motorways are *autoroutes à péage*, toll motorways. You pay at the entrance by throwing coins into a kind of basket or pushing them into a slot, or you are given a ticket and pay at the exit. It is also possible to use credit cards. The motorway network is relatively new in France and very often large sections run parallel to the *routes nationales* (main roads) which are very good and signposted with N followed by a number; D roads are *routes départementales* which are narrower.

Driving in Paris can be very frustrating because of the one-way system and the lack of parking spaces. Parisians have developed an amazing skill at parking in the smallest gap, great use being made of bumpers to enlarge the space between two parked cars. In the centre, most parking spaces are *payant*, with a high hourly rate in an attempt to encourage commuters to use public transport rather than their own cars. August is the only time when driving in Paris is easy – because so many Parisians are away on holiday and parking is free everywhere.

Driving on main roads is best avoided on public holidays during the summer. As most people take their holidays in July or August, on the first and last weekend of these months traffic is at its worst, with long tailbacks near large cities. Statistics for road accidents also warn of danger around the

Hot Tip: Driving on the Périphérique

If you want to avoid driving through Paris, use the *Boulevard Périphérique* (the ring road). However, at peak hours it can be heavily congested, so make sure you stay in the right-hand lane (the slow lane) in order not to miss your exit.

Remember which one you need. If you miss it, use the next one! Many sections of the *Périphérique* were built on what were once the fortifications of Paris, and most exits are called *Porte de. . .* which means 'gate'.

times of the two summer festivals mentioned earlier, 14 July and 15 August since people exchange visits and attend late-night events in a celebratory mood!

In an attempt to reduce drinking and driving, police apply the law rigorously, and driving licences can be withdrawn on the spot.

The police also try and help avoid traffic congestion by suggesting other itineraries. A vast operation called *'bison futé'* invites French holidaymakers to remember their treasure-hunt days and/or be as clever as native American Indians were in finding tracks, by following alternative routes signalled by traffic police with signs of *'bison futé'*, also explained on TV and radio. So play along if you wish to explore an even deeper France than you had bargained for.

The wearing of seatbelts is compulsory and it is illegal to have a child in the front seat either strapped in or on the passenger's lap.

FRENCH RAILWAYS
(SNCF = Societé Nationale des Chemins de Fer)

The SNCF makes great efforts to please customers, besides making sure that trains run on time. Trains are clean and the seats are pleasant and comfortable. In *trains corail* (express trains) there is a special carriage where children can play, and during the summer, entertainment is provided on the main lines at no extra cost. A carriage can house an exhibition, a cinema, become a stage for artists or offer you specialities of the region you are travelling through.

Before boarding a train you must validate your ticket by pushing it into a small machine which punches a hole and stamps the date. (The magic word for this process is 'composter'.) There are frequent ticket inspections on trains and inspectors speak foreign languages, so you cannot easily get away with pretending you do not understand. A hefty fine is levied on the spot from *all* offenders!

In France coaches are not an alternative to trains, they are only used where trains do not go.

All sorts of tariffs and reductions exist. Because trains are so popular, they tend to be crowded at weekends and on public holidays. It is advisable to book in advance in person by Minitel or on the web. It is compulsory to book in advance fot the TGV (*Train à Grande Vitesse*) high-speed train linking Paris to regional capitals and abroad.

'Marianne' (see p. 89)

Hot Tip: Using the Metro

The *Metro* (underground/subway) is the cheapest and fastest way to travel in Paris. Each line takes its name from the last stop, which means that on a return journey the same line will have a different name. If you have to change, follow the sign *Correspondance* and the appropriate name of the line.

It is cheaper to buy a booklet of 10 tickets, so ask for a *carnet*. These tickets can also be used on buses. They can be bought not only at Metro stations but also at newsagents and Cafés-Tabac. On the Metro you only need one ticket whatever the length of your journey and irrespective of the number of times you change lines.

PUBLIC TRANSPORT IN PARIS

(RATP – Régie Autonome des Transports Parisiens – www.ratps.com)

On buses you need one or two tickets according to the length of your journey and you have to pay again whenever you board a new bus. Some bus lines can be a cheap alternative to sightseeing tours as they take you past the main sights. This is true of line 72 between the Hôtel de Ville (Town Hall) and the Eiffel Tower, for example.

Keep your ticket until you leave the bus or Metro as you might be required to produce it for inspection.

The RER (*Réseau Express Régional*) is a mixture of tube and train taking you fast to and from airports, Disneyland, Versailles, and with limited stops at key central points, intersecting with main line stations and the Métro. Several zone prices apply. RER is also managed by RATP. Ask for a map when you buy your first ticket.

Try avoiding the rush hours (between 7.00 and 9.00 in the morning, then 6.00 and 7.30 in the evening) when it would be difficult to extricate yourself and your luggage from the carriage and you would be unpopular with fellow passengers. Push chairs and small luggage are only accepted on buses outside the rush hours. Queuing is virtually unknown at bus stops, so it is necessary to assert yourself.

Public Holidays (*Jours Fériés*)

1 Jan.	New Year's Day	*Jour de l'An*
March/April	Easter Sunday and Easter Monday	*Pâques & Lundi de Pâques*
1 May	Labour Day	*Fête du Travail*
8 May	Victory in Europe Day (end of WW2)	*Fête de la Libération*
Early May (depending on Easter date)	Ascension Day (Christ's)	*Ascension*
Late May	Whitsun Sunday and Monday	*Pentecôte & Lundi de Pentecôte*
14 Jul.	Bastille Day	*Fête Nationale*
15 Aug.	Assumption of the Virgin Mary	*Assomption*
1 Nov.	All Saints' Day	*Toussaint*
11 Nov.	Remembrance Day (end WW1)	*Armistice 1918*
25 Dec.	Christmas Day	*Noël*

9

Out & About

Local open-air market

As in other parts of Europe, large shopping centres and supermarkets are replacing small shops, but French people still rely on corner shops and markets for certain kinds of food. The French like their bread fresh and crisp, and in towns they are prepared to go twice a day to the baker's shop which opens at 7.30 am and remains open until 7.00 or 8.00 pm; it even opens until noon on Sundays. Other shops open later, at 8.00 or 9.00 am, but all of them are shut for two or three hours at midday.

Hot Tip: How to Pay at the Counter

When you pay for goods in France, do not try to put the money directly into the cashier's hands; use the little rubber mat or glass dish on the counter. This is to make sure that there is no disagreement on the amount tendered or the change given back.

POST OFFICES

Hours of business are usually between 8.00 am and 7.00 pm on weekdays and until 12 noon on Saturdays. Stamps can also be obtained from Bars-Tabac. Letter-boxes are yellow.

The public phone system in France is comprehensive and includes even the smallest villages. Coin-operated phones have disappeared, and in large towns most public phones require a *télécarte* (phonecard). If you intend spending some time in France it might be worth buying a *télécarte* with 50 or 100 *unités*. You can buy *télécartes* at post offices,

Fish shop in the heart of Paris

railway stations, Bars-Tabac (with the red carrot sign) and some newsagents. This is to discourage vandalism and theft. Most of the 'télécartes' make attractive souvenirs and some become collectors' items.

As from 1997, the telephone network has been upgraded and made easier, putting every call on a ten-digit number, whether you are making a local or regional call. If you wish to telephone abroad, you now only have to dial 00 + the code for the country. All this is clearly shown inside the street telephone kiosks, with the names of countries, and a map of France showing that Paris and region (Ile de France) now add 01 in front of your correspondent's number, 02 for the North-West, 03 for the North-East, 04 for the South-East and 05 for the South-West.

Check whether you have been given a 10-digit number, in which case you do not need to add anything; if not, a recorded voice will tell you to add one of the above, which will, after all, only test your listening skills up to 5. If you are given a Numéro vert to call, it will start with 008 and it will be free. Most mobile numbers will now show as 06 and there are a few more specialized services with other prefixes.

If you go to a post-office, you are entitled to consult the Minitel free because it replaced book-form directories years ago. It is a type of Internet system. After giving the screen and keyboard free to every household, a huge profit was made on the calls especially to les lignes roses for adult services. You can use your Minitel to book seats on trains, planes and in theatres as well as organize your bank services. Some say its very success slowed down the uptake of Internet provisions, but business and young people are now adept '*internantes*' (net surfers).

BANKS & MUSEUMS

Most banks open between 9.00 am and 12 noon, and from 2.00 pm till 4.00 pm on weekdays; also from 9.30 am to 12 noon on Saturdays. In certain areas they are closed all day on Saturday or Monday. They are closed on Sundays and public holidays. Be aware of the security airlock between the two entrance doors. Press the red button, and when it shows green the door will be unlocked. Repeat for the second door.

Museums and monuments are usually closed all day on Tuesdays. This applies to the main category of 'national' museums. The 'local' ones tend to be closed on Mondays, allowing you, therefore, to plan visits on both days. By far the best way to see what is on as soon as you arrive in Paris is to buy either *Pariscope* or *l'Officiel des spectacles* for about two francs and study it seriously. The prices of the shows are indicated with a bewildering array of reductions for students, pensioners or large families at different times on different days. A list of abbreviations is thankfully to be found before the rubric.

PETROL STATIONS

Sometimes attendants are reluctant to accept cheques or even refuse them for amounts over 100 francs; but credit cards are acceptable.

WHERE TO STAY

The *Office du Tourisme* or *Syndicat d'initiative* (Tourist Information Office) will help you in choosing from a range of hotels rated from one to four stars.

Usually you pay for the room rather than per person, and breakfast is not included. Some hotels which also run restaurants expect you to have a meal there if you want a room, although such a requirement is not legal.

If you wish to stay in a Bed and Breakfast establishment look for the sign *Chambre d'hôtes*. In the countryside *Table d'hôtes* might be on offer as well; this means you can have a meal and take the opportunity to sample local specialities at a reasonable price.

If you plan a longer stay in an area, *gîtes* are an interesting option. These are self-catering holiday homes, very often old farmhouses or houses of character which have been renovated.

Youth Hostels, *Auberges de Jeunesse*, are not generally as numerous as in certain other European countries.

PUBLIC CONVENIENCES

Some public toilets have attendants who will not let you go in unless you put the required amount of money in a little dish. French people are surprised by the reluctance of some foreigners to use *toilettes turques*; they cannot see what all the fuss is about. Instead of having a toilet seat, you stand on slightly raised foot-rests and squat. Just make sure you unlock the door and are ready to exit swiftly before you flush the toilet.

Hot Tip: Using a Public Toilet

The famous free-standing urinals of Paris are now museum pieces and have been replaced by unobtrusive unisex cabins. Green and red lights have replaced the *libre* or *occupé* signs. The door opens when you push coins into a slot. Never go two at a time to save 2F: the automatic cleaning of the whole cublicle starts when the door closes after your exit.

If no public toilets are available, you can go into a café; they will not mind your using their facilities if you leave a tip.

10

Useful Words & Phrases

WORDS YOU ALREADY KNOW

hôtel, restaurant, banque, taxi, poste, téléphone, toilette, bus.

SIGNS

entrée	entrance
déviation	diversion
sortie	exit
péage	toll
interdit	prohibited
douane	Customs

défense de . . .	prohibited
gare	railway station
non fumeur	non-smoking
hommes	gentlemen
femmes	ladies
cédez le passage	give way
vous n'avez pas la priorité	give way
priorité piétons	pedestrians have right of way

WHAT YOU CAN SAY

oui	yes
non	no
pardon	excuse me
bonjour	good morning/day
bonsoir	good evening
au revoir	goodbye
s'il vous plaît	please
parlez-vous anglais?	do you speak English?
comment?	I beg your pardon
je ne comprends pas	I don't understand
où est. . .? où sont	where is. . .?/are?
quand?	when?
c'est combien?	how much is it?
une chambre	a room
avec douche	with shower
avec salle de bain	with bathroom

WHAT YOU MIGHT HEAR

Bon séjour	Have a nice stay
Bon voyage	Have a good journey
Bonne année	Happy New Year
Joyeux Noël	Merry Christmas

French Words Used In This Book

amitié amoureuse 40 — loving friendship

apéritif 56 — before-meal drink taken as an appetizer

Auberges de Jeunesse 82 — Youth Hostels

autoroutes à péage 72 — toll motorways

baptême 47 — baptism, christening

biscotte 54 — toasted bread

boulangerie 57 — baker's shop

Boulevard Périphérique 73 — ring road around Paris & main cities

cadre 30 — executive

carafe d'eau 58 — tap water

carnet 76 — booklet of Metro/bus tickets

Cédez le passage 72 — give way (to traffic on roundabout)

Chambre d'hôtes 82 — Bed and Breakfast

charcuterie 56, 60 — cold meats, sausages, etc.

communion solennelle 47 — First Communion

composter 75 — to validate one's rail ticket in a machine

courriel 70 — e-mail

croque monsieur 66 — ham and cheese toasted sandwich

Défense d'afficher 29 — notices prohibited

départements 14, 15 — administrative districts

Départements d'outre mer (DOM) 13, 14 — overseas districts

Écoles publiques 90 — state schools

entre la poire et le fromage 62 — interval for lively conversation at the end of a meal

Etranger, l' 26 — the outsider

fleuves 15 — major rivers

foie gras *59, 60* — goose or duck liver preserved in own fat

frais de notaire *13* — solicitor's fees

France métropolitaine *13* — the French homeland

France profonde, la *36* — the countryside ('Deep France')

Francophonie, la *38* — French-speaking commonwealth

fromage *66* — cheese

gens du Nord, les *16* — people of Northern France, as perceived by the South

goûter *56* — afternoon snack

Hexagone, l' *13, 14* — term used for France, because of its shape

Hôtel de Ville *76* — Town Hall

internantes *81* — net surfers

jambon *66* — ham

Jours Fériés *77* — Public Holidays

mairie *13* — town hall

Maquis *28* — the Resistance

médecin conventionné *92* — medical practitioner in state scheme

mère patrie, la *13* — mother country

mes sentiments dévoués/les meilleurs *44* — sincere regards/best regards (conventional phrases for ending letters)

Métro, le *76* — the tube, underground railway, subway

métropole, la *13* — mainland France

Midi, le *16* — the South of France

nouveaux riches *22* — new riches

Office du Tourisme *82* — Tourist Information Office

papiers *15* — personal documents

pastis *56* — drink flavoured with aniseed

petites mains *31* — expert seamstresses in fashion houses

porte cochère 52 — entrance to an apartment building

pourboire 66 — tip, gratuity ('for a drink')
Président Directeur Général (PDG) 69 — managing director
prêt-à-porter 32 — ready-to-wear
régions 14 — areas containing groups of départements
réveillon, le 48, 60, 63 — festive, late evening meal at Christmas and New Year

rillette 66 — pork spread
rivières 15 — minor rivers
roi charmeur, le 35 — King Edward VII
Roi Soleil, le 21 — the Sun King (Louis XIV)
routes départementales 73 — secondary roads (B roads)
routes nationales 72 — main roads (A roads)
Saint-Sylvestre, la 60, 63 — New Year's Eve
saucisson 66 — salami
steak saignant/à point/bien cuit/frites 64 — steak rare/medium/well done/and chips
Suze 56 — bitter drink made with herbs

Syndicat d'initiative 82 — Tourist Information Office
télécarte 79 — phonecard
Territoires d'outre mer (TOM) 13 — overseas territories
toite, la 70 — the web
Train à Grande Vitesse (TGV) 75 — high speed train
trains corail 74 — express trains
veuillez agréer 44 — believe me/please accept (preceding complimentary phrase at end of letter)

Vous n'avez pas la priorité 72 — give way (in traffic)

Facts About France

The capital of France is Paris with a population (according to the 1990 census) of 2,152,423 or over nine million if you add in its metropolitan district (MD). Marseilles , the country's most important port, has 800,550 (MD 1.23m), Lyons has 415,487 (MD 1.26m), Lille has 172,142 (MD 0.96m) and Bordeaux has 213,336 (MD 0.7m). Toulouse has 358,688 (MD 0.65m) and is consistently voted as the city with the best quality of life.

Mont Blanc, in the French Alps, is the highest peak in Europe at 4807 metres (15,771 feet).

French Currency

The French currency is the Franc which is equal to 100 centimes. The denominations in notes are 500F, 200F, 100F, 50F and 20F and in coins are 20F, 10F, 5F, 2F, 1F, 50 centimes, 20 centimes, 10 centimes and 5 centimes. Credit cards are widely accepted in France and Travellers' cheques easily cashed.

The Eiffel Tower, which dominates the Parisian skyline, was built in 1887-9 and is 300m (984ft) high.

Marianne

Marianne is the symbol of the French Republic, a female figure found on stamps and coins. Every town hall has a bust of her, sometimes modelled on a famous French woman, from Brigitte Bardot in the sixties to a Chanel model in the eighties. The latest actress chosen for 2000 is causing a scandal by living in London. The French are very upset.

Liberté, Égalité, Fraternité is the motto of the French Republic, which you will see written on public buildings and coins.

Education is compulsory in France between the ages of six and 16.

Most families send their children to state schools (*Écoles publiques*) which are free and considered to provide the best education. The majority go to nursery schools before they reach the compulsory school age of six. Wednesday is a free day for school children but many have lessons on Saturday morning. The French education system is very competitive; children have to repeat a class if they have not achieved a certain level by the end of the school year. The National Curriculum issued by the Ministry of Education prescribes in detail what has to be learned.

Private schools (*écoles privées*) are mainly Roman Catholic and have their own ethos. The curriculum, however, is the same as in state schools as they are under contract to the government which pays the teachers' salaries and contributes to the upkeep of the buildings. Fees are therefore very low and parents tend to choose their children's' schools according to local convenience, reputation and facilities rather than religious feelings.

The French take great pride in their long and prestigious literary tradition. However, in schools, literature is not considered as important as mathematics, an ability which is generally used as a gauge of intelligence, perhaps because it demands skills in logical thinking. Philosophy is compulsory for all students of the 'Bac'.

In higher education, universities are open to anyone who has passed the *Bac(calauréat)* (secondary education leaving certificate) but there is also a system of highly selective *Grandes Écoles* where many future top executives, civil servants and politicians are educated. They are now opening to foreigners to recruit the very best brains and competitive exams (*concours*) can be taken in English.

Every young man over 18 used to have to do military service, although the length of time was being reduced more and more and civil community service could be done instead. Since 1997, boys born after 1979 are called up in front of a commission called *rendez-vous du citoyen*; it will be the same for girls after 2002. The new system enables young people to choose whether to serve in the military or in civic, humanitarian projects for ten months of compulsory SMA (adapted military service). The latest step is that being registered is enough and nobody needs to do any service unless they choose to!

Cycling is very popular. The famous Tour de France race is followed by millions during July. The final stage ends on the Champs Elysées in Paris and the winner wears a yellow vest, the coveted *maillot jaune*.

Boules

In summer, the French like playing *boules*. The aim is to roll solid steel balls as close as possible to a little wooden ball, the *cochonnet* (='piggy'). You can throw them to try and dislodge an opponent's ball. Any patch of ground will do, from a village square to a garden path.

In winter, an increasing number of people go to ski resorts in the Alps or the Pyrénées. Since the law entitles employees to five weeks paid holiday each year, people tend to take three or four weeks in summer, keeping a week or two for a winter break.

France has a long and varied coastline which attracts many holiday-makers who are keen on water sports. But you do not have to be at the seaside to go sailing, water-skiing or windsurfing. Local authorities have made great efforts to develop the potential offered by lakes and have created numerous artificial ones.

In order to attract the tourist industry, regional authorities have renovated waterways which had fallen into neglect when rail and road traffic became more profitable. Hiring a barge or a small boat is now an available option for people who wish to explore a region in an unusual and relaxing way! The 'Canal du Midi' is especially popular.

Légion d'honneur

The Légion d'honneur, created by the Emperor Napoleon, is still one of France's greatest honours. It is conferred for services rendered to the nation. People who have received this honour wear a tiny red ribbon in the shape of a rosette in their lapel.

Your health is important and you are safe in France. The French are great consumers of medical services, certainly by British standards. Do not worry unduly if you are sent for an X-ray; they are just checking that your cold has not reached your chest. It will give you the opportunity of viewing the consultant's antiques in the waiting-room. Alternatively, bring your paracetamols along.

The safest and cheapest way is to go to a chemist's (pharmacie indicated by a green cross outside). They will suggest sensible solutions in case of minor problems or refer you to a doctor's practice, whose details they will have. Make sure you ask for a médecin conventionné who is legally bound to charge you the official rate to be refunded by the sécurité sociale (if you are on E101 from Britain). If you have private insurance, go and admire the antiques. In all cases, keep your receipts. You need not be shy about your health as the French love talking about their illnesses, and gory details of surgery are cheerfully swapped at bus stops. And so,

Bonne chance, Bonne santé, Bon appétit, Bon séjour
Bonnes vacances, Bon voyage
&
A la prochaine!

If you have now developed an appetite for reading about the French because they failed to behave in any way this guide tried to warn you about, you may like to delve into the thousands of pages of facts and figures published in *Quid* updated yearly. Did you know for, instance, that the average height of conscripts enlisted in 1939 was 1.66 metres, while it shot to 1.74 m. in 1980. The helpful suggestion is that the introduction of cycling enabled people to mate further afield, ensuring healthier offspring. Oh là là!

Or you may prefer to try reading the slimmer five hundred-odd pages of *The French*, by Theodore Zeldin, an Englishman who 'knows us better than we know ourselves', or so they say modestly, in such a . . . how shall I put it? – un-French way, maybe!

Index